, to Forgive

seo-hyun jun

forgiveness does not better the bygone
but it is a door to the better for oneself

First paperback edition July 2021

ISBN 979-8-5249-9102-7 (pbk.)

, to Forgive

a poetry book

seo-hyun jun

welcome.

contents

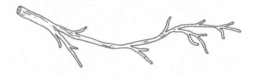

acknowledgements

The atmosphere after closing my laptop after papers and notes that have been around for at least six years or so is exceptionally pleasing in the most grateful way. This book is indeed a small, thin publication of chapters and clumps of words but I would have not been able to produce anything or learn anything as beautiful as poetry without God's grace. For days, a week before sending this work of mine out to the world, I have received countless encouragements and supports from so many of my friends and family members: although written and finalized quietly.

Firstly, my mom, dad, and Danny, being the greatest adventurers in guiding me to design the book, handed me innumerable motivations. Mentioning the designing portion, I would like to honor the four delightful, talented artists and designers I know: Mackenzie Tikkanen, Mariana Perez, Mishio, Alayna Sutherland, and Wardeena Adam. Mishio, I miss immensely, whom I met all the way back in the gorgeous lands of Scotland.

On the side of encouragements, I acknowledge my two smart friends at the gospel hall: Alex Bell and Ryan Belskus. The journeys we had writing and sharing different stories have been such a joy to me.

In closing, I must acknowledge some principal groups of people. One of them would be my grandparents in Korea and my grandparents in America, who have given me so much love since my first day on Earth and I cannot wait to see you all again. Second to last, my amazing seniors whom I have met during the pandemic; the best luck to you all and I will be thinking of each one of you every day. And finally, my fellow activists, the people who I have been working with for three and a half years with immense passion. The ones who truly helped me retrieve my voice, I will never forget.

Seo-Hyun Jun

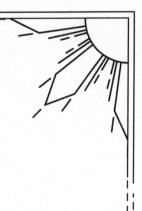

chapter 1.

friendship

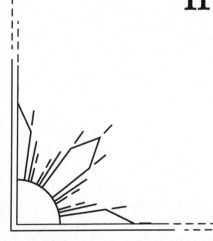

greatest villain

you are the greatest villain on earth, dearest friend.
the precious warmth we shared now trapped in time
meant only a still image to you.

you are the fragile guarding an abyss, dearest friend.
the hours spent blooming my honesty
meant only a gossip to you.

you are the piercing drops of rain, dearest friend.
the weary umbrella i was against your enemies
meant only an ornament to you.

you are the deepest of the sea, dearest friend.
i could not find you when drowning to the lowest.

it takes pain and courage to admit that
you are, however,
the person i will miss grandly, dearest friend.

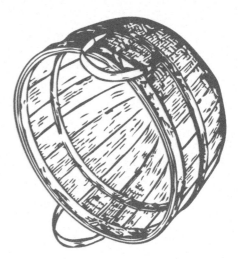

blue oranges

we ran together into a field.
a bright field i thought.

"can oranges be blue?"
you say yes although you have no clue.

we take a bite.
a sweet and sour taste i thought.

"can oranges be salty?"
you say yes although these ones are faulty.

we put them in the basket.
you take some of mine to yours.

"your oranges are bluer than mine."
oh dear, but those quite malign.

i picked the ones so ugly
for you to be the best divine.

come on back, let's pick some more
before i see you nevermore.

stardust

eight,
we watched the stardust together.
"let's go to outer space," we said.

twelve,
we watched the stardust together.
"let's build a spaceship," we said.

seventeen,
white stardust on your desk.
"want to do it together?" you ask.

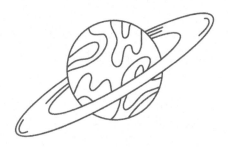

the red sun on our nose
your red eyes in the dark.

"will we ever be astronauts?" i ask.
"what do you mean?" you laugh.

nothing, sister, nothing.
i meant i don't want to lose you.

intertwine

our first conversation in a decade
and i can only say so many.

i have looked everywhere.
i no longer wear the bracelet
on my wrist
you made me eleven years ago.
it makes me small
to see it still shine in hope on yours.

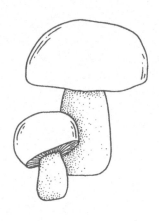

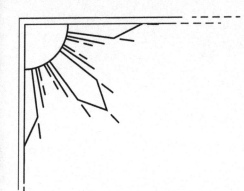

chapter 2.

family

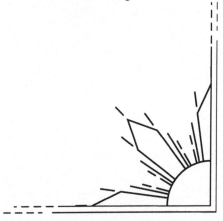

my dream dress

this week whizzed by so quickly.

on monday i was barely four feet tall.
i pulled her pinkie as i reached out
for that chiffon dress
i could wear to school.
a cold "no" she gave.

on wednesday i was almost five feet tall.
i pulled her hand as i reached out
for that silk dress
i could wear to the show.
a cold "no" she gave.

on friday i was now over five feet tall.
i pulled her arm as i reached out
for that velvet dress
i could wear to the party.
a cold "no" she gave.

on sunday i was ready and steady,
i pulled her heart as i craved for that yes,
and i reached out for that lacy dress
i could wear down the aisle.
a happy "yes" she gave.

metamorphosis

the woman wept in bliss
and the caterpillar slept softly on her chest.
the woman's eyes were all about affection
but thus was in fine gradation
with a flaming spirit of a warrior;
she would die for the tiny caterpillar.
in months, it transformed into colors of awe.
"a butterfly!" she gasped.

but the lovely insect flew away in haste
as it saw the woman was giant compared to its size.
the woman desperately screamed for its return
but the butterfly was too far
and already up in its world of misdeeds.
it could hear her faint cry and
"my baby" it was.

few scenes of your mouth forming shapes
a question formed with pure betrayal
comes to mind
why can you not understand
my tears are worth as yours
and have reason

window

le rêveur

i once imagined dragons and invisible cloaks
wherever i went.

they only stayed for a few years or so.

because the moment i found the bravery
to walk home from school alone,
"too much of a dreamer,"
my parents would note.

those were bitter words but yes,
the reality was too cruel at times
for the dragons and the invisible cloaks to be true.

even so, i am much of a born dreamer.
i dream everyday of
having the finest abilities
to possibly thank my parents
as much as their sacrifices.

the petals on her body

i had a dream one night.
i met a lady in a green shirt.
she asked what was my favorite thing to do.
i said writing.

she insisted i write her story one day,
so here it is.

i, then, a nine year old, grew up in fame.
my mother was a known smoker
and my father was a known drinker.
the sound of the car would be my hint to dart.

if slow, i would be his canvas.
the red on my skin would later be purple.
mother, soaked in sweat
would whisper with a faint smirk,
"you've got some pretty petals on you."
petals, she said.

petals.

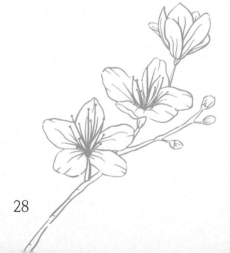

chapter 3.

relationship &
intimacy

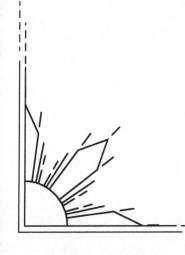

pepperoni pizza

growing up, i never liked pepperonis.
it wasn't particularly the flavor
yet its imbalanced chemistry with cheese
was a disturbance, i'd say.
like so, all of the pepperonis on my pizza
would go to my brother.

one observation any can make
when one is in immature love
is that the pepperoni-hater starts to
no longer hate pepperonis.
no matter how terrible it may be in the mouth,
the pepperoni-hater chews it and gulps it down
with a huge smile on their face
to impress their most important, diamond-like lover.

the second observation that any can make is that the
"most important, diamond-like lover" does not care.
surely, the lover may treasure the beauty and the body.
not the pepperoni-hater's efforts
to eat the pepperoni, though.

later on,
the pepperoni-hater ended up favoring the ham
whether or not the "immature love"
left a deep scar in her.

well,
pepperonis are somewhat nice, i guess.

mr. darcy

a ball with people rich and poor
all over with the old and young.

was it his pride or the family of hers
that filled the air with hostile words?

was he too arrogant or she too ignorant
towards the love now too permanent?

enough, elizabeth! i love too ardently
i refuse to age alone as a rotten tree.

the ugly in me not prettier than yours
our tied knot would be the proof of it all.

but this is their story now let us mend ours
the truth be unveiled after the flowers.

enough with resentment and talks over fortune,
or eyes against one's maturity,

confirm with all certainty for one small request:
that you be my darcy and i your lizzy.

a somber music
with unvarnished lyrics.

i promise,
if i could quiet the creature in me,
i would.

no need to run from me darling,
isn't it an acoustic.

doloroso

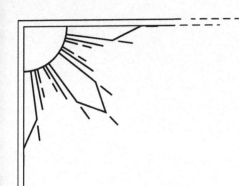

chapter 4.

myself

turning twenty

was told three years now
decides thirty years 'morrow
but i feel thirteen

20.

a lost sheep

Lord, I want the sweetest chocolates in the town.
    Newly in the market, my child.

Lord, I want a juicy, homemade apple pie.
    In your aunt's hands, my child.

Lord, I want chicken nuggets glistened with sauce.
    By the corner of this block, my child.

Lord, today I want nothing.
    Why is that, my child?

Because, Lord.
I want to be Ava, she is so pristine.
I want to be Giselle, she is flawless.
Will you tell me where I can be them?
    But child, you are complete, unblemished, sublime...

Lord, I want freshly baked glazed donuts.

belle

they placed me as common
but why be so
when i hold
the wit
the capability
the charm
and the possession.

personal color

i paint myself with red and blue.
red for the spots i do not like,
blue for the spots i do like.

i painted.

my body was red.

why so red?

the fat under my arms and thighs,
the dots over my body,
the double chin and acne.

yes, countless of reasons here and there
but i think you and i both know
we look better in blue.

ms. jenkins

in third grade,
a little boy across the classroom may have yelled,

"ms. jenkins, i don't want to sit next to her!"

whatever it was
my accent, my clothes, or my awkward handshake

they were swans and i was an ugly duck.

so then, i wished my differences could be similarities.

i now wish
i did not wish for it.

chapter 5.

the world

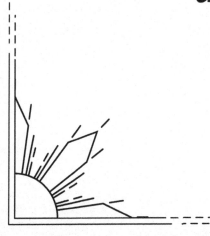

the fifties of korea
in a building to learn
two sisters sat next to my grandpa
without a heated box.
he gave them his rice
in his heated box
and the bodies in resent
from the vile war after their losses
were now beginning to eat
for some wondrous ambitions.

heated boxes

apocalypse

tied and clutched
her brown skin he brushed
then in a cage he tossed
drinking rose water in trust
good money he thought
on the stage he cut
the ribbons so puffed
and in front they watched
faces white and blushed
her feature in lust
then came in so blunt
a face of disgust
no human they grunt
a zombie dont touch
in the water she plunged
to her home she walked
her people they shushed
im a woman she gushed
no a zombie they rushed.

18 miles from my town
28% of alcohol
and a girl born 8 years ago
went through 80 minutes of torture
80000 seconds of injustice
but just 4380 days of suffering for him
while her family in agony for infinity and more

a cursed mercy

brainless trend

stripes this morning
polkadots this afternoon
and florals this evening
i'd rather an invisible cloak

the given tree

the giving tree from our childhood
it has offered us
apples
shades
and memories
we repaid it with a chopped bark
cease the taking
for the given is not deathless

reciprocation

"do not treat me like an animal"
so you are mindful of how they are treated
seized imprisoned and whipped

humans are spoiled animals
breathing hypocrisy
throning ferocity as virtue

the silent

a fruit dove
which has spread its wings through all:
the once majestic
forests deserts waters and icebergs
cried its final song

mourn for us
as we fade into dirt

lines

it invades human land
it dies
human invades its land
it dies
it walks inside borders
although it is outside the bars

the author

Seo-Hyun (Sunny) Jun is a Korean author, poet, full-time student, and activist. She was born in Seoul, South Korea, and is now a high school senior in Michigan. In both her city and county, she is a representative in the youth commission. At her school, she is the founder and a member of multiple organizations and clubs that advocates for women's education, racial equality, and cultural appreciation.

Made in the USA
Columbia, SC
16 July 2021